Also by Barbara Bush

Your Own True Colors

Barbara Bush

Commencement Address
Wellesley College
June 1, 1990

SCRIBNER

New York   London   Toronto   Sydney   New Delhi

SCRIBNER

An Imprint of Simon & Schuster, Inc.

1230 Avenue of the Americas

New York, NY 10020

First Scribner hardcover edition June 2018

SCRIBNER and design are registered trademarks of The Gale Group, Inc.,
used under license by Simon & Schuster, Inc., the publisher of this work.

For information about special discounts for bulk purchases,
please contact Simon & Schuster Special Sales at 1-866-506-1949
or business@simonandschuster.com.

The Simon & Schuster Speakers Bureau can bring authors to your live event.
For more information or to book an event, contact the Simon & Schuster Speakers
Bureau at 1-866-248-3049 or visit our website at www.simonspeakers.com.

Interior illustrations by Taylor Noel

Interior design by Erich Hobbing

Manufactured in the United States of America

1   3   5   7   9   10   8   6   4   2

Library of Congress Cataloging-in-Publication Data is available.

ISBN 978-1-9821-0951-6

ISBN 978-1-9821-0953-0 (ebook)

YOUR OWN
TRUE COLORS

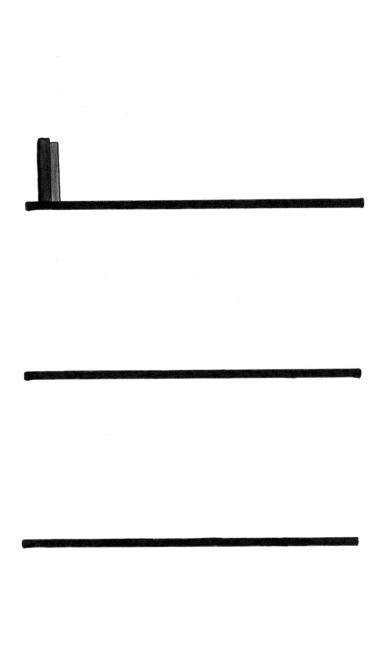

More than ten years ago when I was first invited to speak at Wellesley, I was struck by both the natural beauty of your campus . . . and the spirit of this place.

Wellesley, you see, is not just a place . . . but an idea . . . an experiment in excellence in which diversity is not just tolerated, but is embraced.

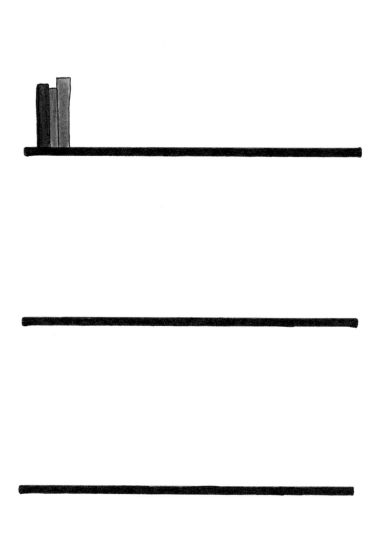

The essence of this spirit was captured in a moving speech about tolerance given by the Student Body President of one of your sister colleges. She related the story by Robert Fulghum about a young pastor who, finding himself in charge of some very energetic children, hit upon a game called "Giants, Wizards, and Dwarfs."

"You have to decide now," the Pastor instructed the children, "which you are . . . a giant, a wizard, or a dwarf?"

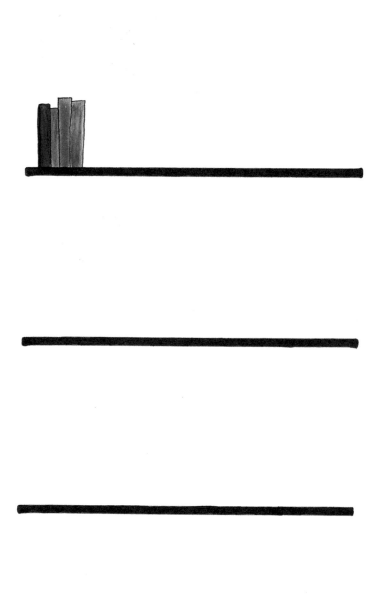

At that, a small girl tugging on his pant leg asked, "But where do the mermaids stand?"

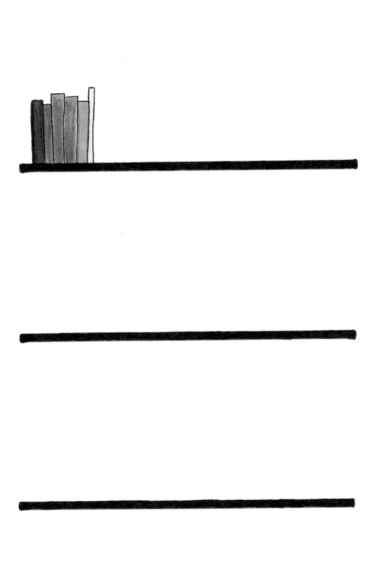

The Pastor told her there are *no* mermaids. "Oh yes there are," she said. "I am a mermaid."

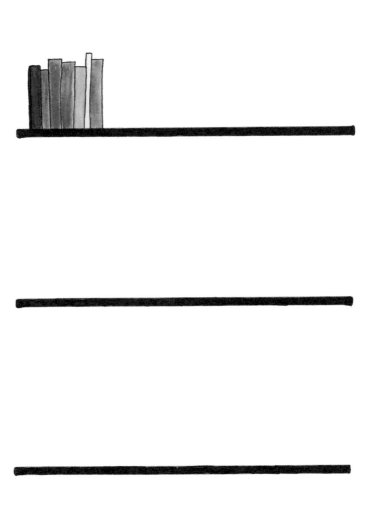

This little girl knew what she was. She was not about to give up on either her identity *or* the game. She intended to take her place wherever mermaids fit into the scheme of things.

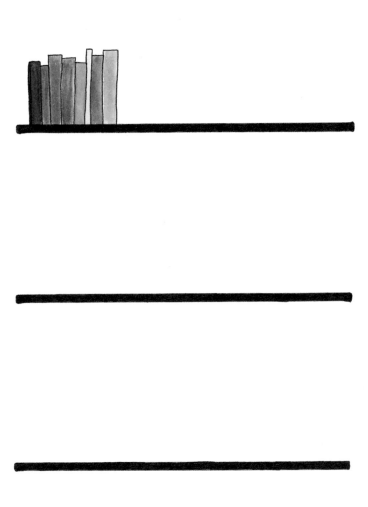

Where *do* mermaids stand . . . all those who are different, those who do not fit the boxes and the pigeonholes? "Answer that question," wrote Fulghum, "and you can build a school, a nation, or a whole world on it."

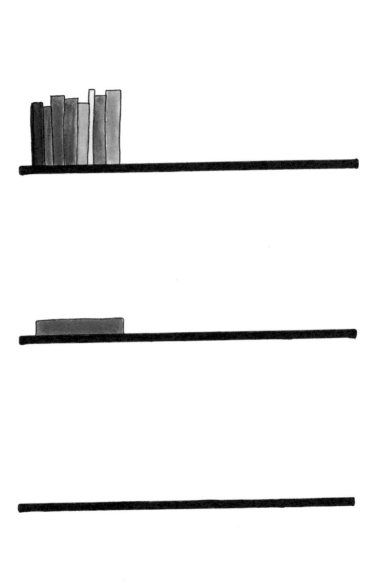

As that very wise young woman said, "Diversity . . . like anything worth having . . . requires *effort*." Effort to learn about and respect difference, to be compassionate with one another, to cherish our own identity . . . and to accept unconditionally the same in all others. You should all be very proud that this is the Wellesley spirit.

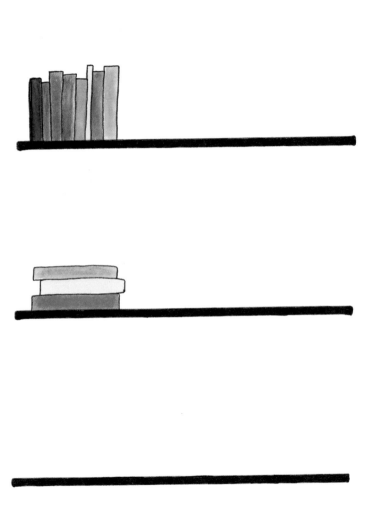

Now I know your first choice for today was Alice Walker, known for *The Color Purple.* Instead you got me—known for . . . the color of my hair! Of course, Alice Walker's book has a special resonance here. At Wellesley, each class is known by a special color . . . and for four years the class of '90 has worn the color purple.

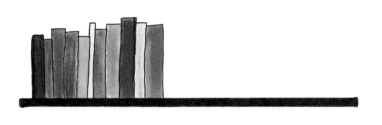

Today you meet on Severance Green to say good-bye to all that . . . to begin a new and very personal journey . . . a search for your own true colors.

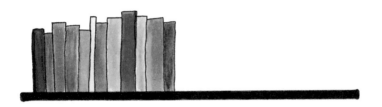

In the world that awaits you beyond the shores of Lake Waban, no one can say what your true colors will be. But this I know: You have a first-class education from a first-class school. And so you need not, probably cannot, live a "paint-by-numbers" life.

Decisions are not irrevocable. Choices do come back. As you set off from Wellesley, I hope that many of you consider making three very special choices.

The first is to believe in something larger than yourself . . . to get involved in some of the big ideals of your time.

I chose literacy because I honestly believe that if more people could read, write, and comprehend, we would be that much closer to solving so many of the problems plaguing our society.

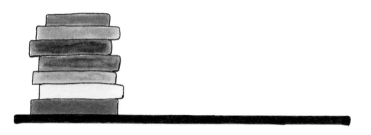

Early on I made another choice which I hope you will make as well. Whether you are talking about education, career, or service, you are talking about life . . . and life must have joy. It's supposed to be fun!

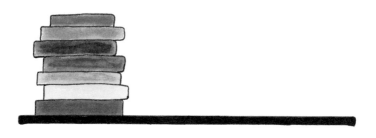

One of the reasons I made the most important decision of my life . . . to marry George Bush . . . is because he made me laugh. It's true, sometimes we've laughed through our tears . . . but that shared laughter has been one of our strongest bonds.

Find the joy in life, because as Ferris Bueller said on his day off . . . "Life moves pretty fast. Ya don't stop and look around once in a while, ya gonna miss it!"

The third choice that must not be missed is to cherish your human connection: your relationships with friends and family.

For several years, you've had impressed upon you the importance to your career of dedication and hard work. This is true, but as important as your obligations as a doctor, lawyer, or business leader will be, you are a human being first, and those human connections—with spouses, with children, with friends—are the most important investments you will ever make.

At the end of your life, you will never regret not having passed one more test, not winning one more verdict, or not closing one more deal. You will regret time not spent with a husband, a friend, a child, or a parent.

We are in a transitional period right now . . .
fascinating and exhilarating times . . . learning
to adjust to the changes and the choices we . . .
men and women . . . are facing.

I remember what a friend said, on hearing her husband lament to his buddies that he had to baby-sit. Quickly setting him straight . . . my friend told her husband that when it's your own kids . . . it's not called baby-sitting!

Maybe we should adjust faster, maybe slower. But whatever the era . . . whatever the times, one thing will never change: fathers and mothers, if you have children . . . they must come first. Your success as a family . . . our success as a society . . . depends *not* on what happens at the White House, but on what happens inside your house.

For over fifty years, it was said that the winner of Wellesley's Annual Hoop Race would be the first to get married. Now they say the winner will be the first to become the CEO. Both of these stereotypes show too little tolerance for those who want to know where the mermaids stand.

So I offer you today a new legend: The winner of the hoop race will be the first to realize her dream . . . not society's dream . . . her own personal dream.

And who knows? Somewhere out in this audience may even be someone who will one day follow in my footsteps, and preside over the White House as the President's spouse. I wish him well!

The controversy ends here. But our conversation is only beginning. And a worthwhile conversation it is. Thank you. God bless you. And may your future be worthy of your dreams.

ABOUT THE AUTHOR

Barbara Bush (1925–2018) was born in
Rye, New York, and married George H. W.
Bush in 1945. She served as First Lady of the
United States from 1989 to 1993. She has five
children—including President George W. Bush
and Florida Governor Jeb Bush—seventeen
grandchildren, and eight great-grandchildren.
She founded the Barbara Bush Foundation for
Family Literacy. She lived in Houston, Texas, and
Kennebunkport, Maine.